Crap
Dates

Crap Dates

Disastrous Encounters from Single Life

Rhodri Marsden

CHRONICLE BOOKS
SAN FRANCISCO

First published in the United States in 2013
by Chronicle Books.

First published in the United Kingdom in 2012
by Simon & Schuster UK Ltd.

Text copyright © 2012 by Rhodri Marsden.

Library of Congress Cataloging-in-Publication Data
Marsden, Rhodri.
  Crap dates : disastrous encounters from single life / Rhodri Marsden.
     pages cm
  ISBN 978-1-4521-1458-3
1. Dating (Social customs)--Humor. I. Title.

  PN6231.D3M3655 2013
  818'.60208--dc23

                        2013001829

Manufactured in China

Designed and illustrated by Walter C. Baumann

All tweets are associated exclusively with Twitter, Inc.

10 9 8 7 6 5 4 3

Chronicle Books LLC
680 Second Street
San Francisco, California 94107
www.chroniclebooks.com

This book is dedicated to everyone who's been on a crap date . . . particularly if it was with me.

When it goes well, a date can be exhilarating.

An improbable spark suddenly fires, both of you realize that you have a connection above and beyond your favorite brand of dishwasher tablet, and invisible hearts start popping in the air around you.

But it's not always like that. In fact, if we're going to be honest, it's hardly ever like that. And the more dates we go on (via newspaper ads, Internet sites, speed dating, and inappropriate blind dates set up by friends predisposed to cruelty) the higher the failure rate. That's not me being cynical, I promise—it's just statistics.

Yes, in theory, a period of relentless dating might improve your chances of meeting someone wonderful, but it mainly establishes a long line of people for you to spend disappointing evenings with while you wait for the right person to come along.

There's a positive outcome to emerge from the crammed diary of the hopeful singleton, however, and that's the extraordinary stockpile of anecdotes detailing all the times it went badly wrong. Whether you disliked the other person, they disliked you, or you found some kind of grim solidarity in your mutual loathing, that unique and acute social discomfort becomes seared into your memory. The stories become dinner party staples as your grim experiences, mellowed by time, transform into comedy gold.

As I walked down the A24 in Clapham one Tuesday evening last year, I passed a bar that brought one dating memory of my own flooding back. It was from 2002—the very early days of Internet dating, a thrilling new social experiment as yet untainted by despondent cynicism. This girl and I quickly realized that we had nothing in common, save for speaking English and being a bit lonely. We were doomed to spend a long, excruciating evening together, and the silences became yawning chasms. She was from Wigan, a town in Greater Manchester, and I actually heard myself saying, in a moment of barrel-scraping desperation: "So, what's Wigan like, then?"

I'd gotten into the habit of posting idle thoughts on Twitter rather than keeping them to myself, and that's what I did that Tuesday evening: the story of my bad date, cut back to 140 characters. A couple of people sent theirs back, and I reposted them. Soon, the combined wit of the Twitter community generated a glorious stream of tweets, a cathartic explosion of storytelling. Stripped of extraneous detail, they became brilliantly funny one-liners, haiku-like in their beauty. This collection of stories went viral; by the end of that week a quarter of a million people across the world had come to read them and, in many cases, share their own.

A couple of trends immediately became apparent. First, there were far more stories from women than from men. I'm still not sure whether this is because women are more open about revealing their bad romantic experiences, or that men are just more badly behaved. But judging by the evidence contained within this book, I have a sneaking suspicion it's the latter. Second, the stories from Britain seemed, to me at least, to be the most potent—perhaps because we're more socially inept, more apologetic, more likely to put up with rudeness and idiocy than our North American, Australian, or South African counterparts.

Some of the tales in this book are simply funny, some are shocking, but they're all laced with poignancy. All the storytellers went on their dates with the most honorable of intentions: they were lured by the promise of eventual romance, be it light jazz and croissants on a Sunday morning, or leaping out of a plane strapped to someone gorgeous. The search for love might well be a lottery, or stacked Jenga-like against us, but we always remain hopeful; we'd all like to be with someone, but that person simply hasn't showed up yet. Dating is about hope. And when hope is cruelly shattered, a wistful tale is born.

Of course, if you meet someone fantastic, there isn't really much of a story to tell. What you're doing and where you're doing it almost fails to register. The evening slips by as effortless conversation flows, synergy is established, moments of hysterical mirth are shared. But most of the time, dating is—as a friend of mine once said—a load of single people, of varying degrees of loneliness, blundering about with their arms out hoping to bump into someone. I fervently believe that we'll all blunder and subsequently bump into the right person eventually. But in the meantime, as we keep blundering, let's keep reassuring each other that it's not us with the problem. It's them. ♥

GENERAL
HEARTBREAK

THE SNAPPY
DRESSER

THE ARROGANT
SCUMBAG

THE MAMA'S
BOY

THE OVERBEARING
DICTATOR

THE BLATANT
LIAR

THE CHIVALROUS
GENTLEMAN

THE EXHAUSTING
DULLARD

THE MARRIED
MAN

THE PERSISTENT
STALKER

THE UNHINGED
DRUNKARD

THE DISGRUNTLED
DUMPEE

THE MACHO
POSER

THE DISAPPEARING
ACT

THE PARTY
ORGANIZER

THE SINISTER
CREEP

THE SEXUAL
DEVIANT

THE TACTLESS
IDIOT

THE DELUDED
OPTIMIST

THE TIMID
CREATURE

THE CHARMLESS
CHEAPSKATE

It was going well until we got to the club, she started doing what can only be described as the "pooing on the floor" dance.

We disagreed about something superfluous. She said "This relationship is not working, you have to agree to everything I say."

She asked to see my iPod. After the click of the scroll wheel and raised eyebrows, we parted.

He said: "From your photo I thought you were too good for me, I'm glad to see that you've got flaws." Then he listed them.

He told me my hands were "so beautiful" then he said the painting was "so beautiful" then a lamp, a book cover. He was stoned.

A 23 yr old girl. "I think for my age I've achieved a hell of a lot." she said. Then talked for three hours about her internet business.

#THE SNAPPY DRESSER

I went on a blind date wearing a bright pink blazer and jeans. I turned up to find him wearing exactly the same thing.

In theory, there's someone for everyone. But because first impressions count, there may not be someone for that person who shows up for a date wearing overalls. We make dress code blunders almost despite ourselves, as nerves skew our idea of what constitutes sensible clothing. We might spend hours getting ready and still make elementary mistakes, like leaving the house wearing moccasins, or sweatbands, or chain mail, or all three. Overthinking an outfit might cause someone to turn up bedecked in Hawaiian garlands, or sporting seventeenth-century French court attire. They should really have asked someone who wasn't suffering from acute anxiety whether they looked all right. And maybe glued the sole of their shoe back on.

He asked me: "If you had to choose, who would you rather sleep with—your mom or your dad?"

He read me a four-page poem about a girl who wasn't me. He read it twice as I'd failed to give it enough attention the first time.

@stevefarris24

Went back to her place. Dave Matthews pictures all over her apartment. She showed me her shoulder tattoo: Dave Matthews. I left.

 @Feliskitty

After the date I rejected him. He burst into tears, said he loved me, then turned up outside my work, crying, every day for a week.

We watched *Alien vs. Predator.* Turns to me and says "I don't believe women should be in a position of power."

My date told me I looked quite attractive, from a certain angle.

Met him at his apartment. He opened the door in a blue-check fleece dressing gown and an electronic tag on his ankle. "Shall we just stay in?"

He told me he found it odd to be dating someone "a couple of rungs down the ladder to what he was used to."

He spent the entire date explaining how he would "do" me on our next date, complete with body motions. It was porno charades.

He talked nonstop of how he suspected that his uncle had killed his aunt, he just needed proof.

#THE ARROGANT SCUMBAG

@AFMJen

"I don't want to go out with you again, but we can be friends. Maybe grab a drink and I can tell you why I don't want to date you."

A date is a delicate balancing act. If one person seems far more eager than the other, the whole thing can be irretrievably ruined. But the arrogant scumbag dooms things right away by operating on the assumption that you're thrilled to be in their company, and will make this abundantly clear by scolding you like an errant intern who's behind on their photocopying duties. If they don't like you, they'll go through the process of letting you know why, oblivious to their own failings, which are lit up in neon and flashing rapidly. If they do like you, they'll patiently explain the terms under which they'd be prepared to engage in a relationship. "You'll be pleased to hear that I've accepted you for the vacant post." Um, forget it.

I once told a date a joke and delivered the punchline just as he took a sip of wine. He spat a whole mouthful of Chianti in my face.

A pilot. He said he was married but flew to Amsterdam sometimes, and was interested in me because I was "geographically convenient."

Both me and her turned up at different entrances, stood there for 30 minutes before going home assuming the other had stood us up.

Took a cute guy home and slept with him. In the morning I went for a shower, and came out to find him masturbating into my shoe.

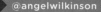
@angelwilkinson

He asked me "How long until you get the menopause?"

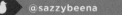
@sazzybeena

I accidentally texted "This one's a bit cocky" to the date who was buying me a drink, instead of my friend.

@sazzybeena

He leant across the table, dragged his fingers through my hair and said "Don't EVER cut your hair."

Halfway through the first date, he leaned forward and asked me if he was making me "gooey" in my "wee-wee."

My blind date had said he looked like Harrison Ford. Me: "You look nothing like Harrison Ford." Him: "Shall we leave it then?"

@kwoodate

We went on a hike in the woods. He killed a bunch of tadpoles, and farted when he tried to pull a stick out of some mud.

 @chrisbell

First date with a woman, who got really angry when people asked if we were on a first date. We're both now married to people called Helen.

# #THE MAMA'S BOY

I was once asked if I would, and I quote, "rub my bottom like Mommy used to."

There are those in the dating pool who haven't managed to sever the parental umbilical cord and are struggling with their identity as an adult. There are a few signs to look out for: for example, they may turn up carrying plush toys, insist on drinking through a novelty straw, and depart on a tricycle. For once, the most likely offenders in this category are women—Daddy's Girls tend to make liberal use of the words "itsy-bitsy" or "drinkie-winkie," or phrases like "I have to go tinkle" that would chill any normal person to the core. But men are by no means off the hook; be exceptionally wary of the ones who shout "Mommy!" at inopportune moments, such as when the bill arrives, when trying to hail a taxi, or at the point of orgasm.

He asked me if I needed the loo, as I'd crossed my legs. Then he told a story about him attacking a guy in the school showers with his own shit.

Met a guy for lunch. He phoned 43 times that evening, rang directory assistance, got my parents' number and asked my Dad if he could marry me.

#THE OVERBEARING DICTATOR

He told me how to manage my finances. When I said I'd make my own decisions, he screamed at me and stormed off the bus.

It's normal for slightly dominant or submissive roles to develop within the context of a long-term relationship, but to start ruling with an iron rod within minutes of meeting someone is a bad assumption to make, and a dangerous strategy to take. Phrases indicating a potential boot-camp scenario include "No, not like that, like this," "I would have appreciated being consulted in advance," and the classic "We will either do things my way, or not at all." Grammar pedants would do well to rein in their compulsion to correct "that" for "which" (or "less" for "fewer") until some kind of rapport has been firmly established. Persistent criticism of the most undermining kind should be saved up for the second day of your honeymoon.

He turned up at my place carrying a man-bag. He made constant references to his hand-axe that he said would fit perfectly in said bag.

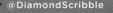

I mentioned that I like *Anchorman*, so he started to quote whole scenes. Standing up, in a quiet pub. I no longer like *Anchorman*.

@FM_Mandog

He asked me if I believed in "Stockholm Syndrome."

@alisonrevitt

He wanted me to pretend we'd been a couple for years, then demanded "Tell me you love me!"

@TakinOutTheTash

"I work in oil and gas, what do you do?" "I work for an environmental protection agency." "Oh."

We bumped into my dad. He took one look at my date, looked at me and said: "You've got to be joking, Lorna."

#THE BLATANT LIAR

He pretended to be a doctor. When busted, he pretended that he was a secret agent posing as a doctor.

Internet dating doesn't encourage truthfulness. Competitive site members describe themselves as younger, taller, thinner, more widely travelled, more successful and more into bungee jumping than they actually are—and the first date is where the wheels start to come off. While attempting to ingratiate themselves via a scattershot process of second-guessing, this category of dater might state that they love dogs, are allergic to dogs, or enjoy eating dogs within the space of three minutes. They pointlessly try to tick boxes that don't need ticking, forgetting that even if their story about being Dustin Hoffman's nephew impresses in the short term, the truth will eventually emerge in a hideously embarrassing denouement.

We meet at the cinema.
I wait at the end of the stairs.
He walks up, sees me, turns
around and walks away :(

He asked me if he could
watch me wee as it turns
him on. I left immediately.

She dragged me round various houseware stores and critiqued the items on sale in agonizing detail.

A blind date. He turned out to be a weirdo who didn't order anything but watched me eat then paid for it.

His opening gambit: "I have a treacherous mind." Byeeee!

He got mad when I didn't finish my dinner, then informed me we were going to smoke weed (I'm allergic to weed) in a cemetery.

After many awkward silences, I actually heard myself say: "So, do you buy anything on eBay?"

He told me that the night before he had pissed in the underwear drawers of his three female housemates, and was I put off? Yes.

On a long drive to Pizza Hut he told me all about the meaning of Phil Collins' "In the Air Tonight" while playing it on repeat.

He got hammered, pissed against a tree in a park and proceeded to tackle me to the ground in my skirt when my back was turned.

He suggested I shag him: "You might as well, I'm going to tell people we slept together anyway." I declined. He was true to his word.

#THE CHIVALROUS GENTLEMAN

He refused to walk me to a taxi in town at 3 am because "statistically, I'm more likely to be attacked than you."

Medieval knights were obliged by a code of honor to "do nothing to displease maidens," but times have changed. Some men, their brains clouded by a shitstorm of confused logic based on an article about feminism that they once half-digested, won't even bother showing common courtesy because they figure it's no longer necessary. No woman is expecting a bloke to take off his jacket and place it over a muddy puddle, but they'd rather he didn't stomp in the puddle hard, while laughing. Or tell her to mop it up. A generation of men is now growing up who will greet the sound of a shrill fire alarm by fleeing for the nearest exit and leaving their date to be consumed by the raging inferno. From such incidents blossoms precious little romance.

He got so incredibly drunk that he confessed to wanking his brother off when he was 11. I ran.

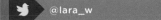

He drove me three times around the block so I could fully admire the walnut dashboard on his new Jag. It was a five minute walk.

It was supposed to be a group of people. Those other people didn't exist.

I went on a date with a guy who depressed us both by talking about how he killed cows organically for a summer job. He cried.

@forkncorka

The first Irish girl I went out with pops up 40 minutes late, no apology, just says "I really hate your tie."

@WastedElegance

He didn't know my name, didn't buy one drink and spat in front of me in the street. Later he texted me asking what underwear I was wearing.

@GlossCommsPR

My friend went on a date with a man who asked if he could pay to watch her do his ironing.

#THE EXHAUSTING DULLARD

@TrayboMcC

The date was so bad that when he called afterwards I said I couldn't talk as I was watching **Crocodile Dundee.**

It's like watching an insufferably tedious television program while strapped tightly to a chair and the remote control lying on a table about three feet out of reach. You can't change the channel. You're stuck with an analysis of the recent application of fiscal stimuli to the Namibian economy, a rundown of the current bestselling dishwashers, or insight into the thought processes of a stick insect. Your facial expression of total indifference, boredom, and frustration will be interpreted as a curious fascination, as they go on to present you with relevant pamphlets and a souvenir DVD. Those who don't date regularly may think that this kind of banality isn't as bad as sitting in total silence, but to be honest I'm not convinced that's true.

I met him at his place as he had "someone for me to meet." It was his teddy bear, of whom he had hundreds of photos on the walls as well.

He took half my meal as he said I'd had enough already. He farted loudly all way home. He thought we'd get on as he "liked cats too."

He left the table to go and vomit after every course. Said he was training. I don't remember what for.

I met a bloke for what was supposed to be lunch. He told me he didn't like what I was wearing, and said I should go home and change.

I once had a date go horribly bad when I got drunk and pointed out that the Smiths' lyrics tattooed on her arm were wrong.

@ olifranklin

My date got a text from a mutual friend during drinks: "Has he talked about the Rwandan genocide yet?" Worse, the answer was yes, I had.

@ heiditretheway

He answered his mobile three times. To talk to his ex-fianceé. About the house they were remodeling. Together. Still.

I turned up. He stood there with cue cards and "spoke" through them, Bob Dylan-style, before he'd "let" me hear his voice.

She checked if I had washed hands after going to the toilet, told me off for restaurant choice, and phoned afterwards to ask what had gone wrong.

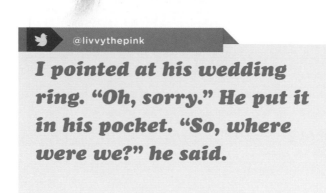

#THE MARRIED MAN

I pointed at his wedding ring. "Oh, sorry." He put it in his pocket. "So, where were we?" he said.

Men supposedly have a genetic predisposition to mate with as many women as possible, but attempts to satisfy this urge are inevitably characterized by anger, jealousy, awkward social situations, and a bunch of laughable excuses. Nevertheless, men of all sorts still try it on, relentlessly, and women have been known to make similar errors. Perhaps you're trapped in a relationship where romance has been replaced by TV nights, home improvements, and golf—so you make a calculated decision to embark upon a doomed fling. Preferably with someone gullible enough not to question why you start sweating every time your mobile phone rings, or wonder why you keep calling them by someone else's name and then apologizing.

Had date with a yogi. He bought me an ice cream, took me to see his Buddha shrine, told me he'd taken a vow of celibacy, then jumped me.

He invited me to his house for dinner. He ordered pizza and made me watch him play online Bingo.

I'd fancied him for a while. On our first (and last) date he told me his hobby was eating paper, then demonstrated with the local news.

As a conversation opener, she showed me 25 photos she'd taken of Sylvia Plath's grave.

@digmy_mood

A date showed up with an albino ferret named Dylan on a leash. She channeled all chat through him. "Dylan says . . ."

We played that game, "I've never ..." I asked him if he'd ever been arrested. "Yes, seven times actually, twice for attempted murder."

Before sitting down, he announced: "I'm Jon, I don't want kids or commitment," then went to the bathroom.

#THE PERSISTENT STALKER

He drank a LOT & talked about his sister a LOT. I left and he phoned 20+ times. The last voicemail was him singing Billy Ocean at 4 am.

They don't take "no" for an answer. In fact, they see "no" as an opportunity for further negotiation. "No" is something these people can work with. Needy, but also in possession of vast reserves of self-belief, they continue to pursue you after a terrible date, convinced that their behavior is "romantic" when it's in fact an arrestable offence. When you don't respond to their excitable text, they send another to ask if you received their excitable text. The thing is, even if they were able to change your mind, it would never be achieved by relentless nagging. They would need to make wholesale changes to their personality and appearance, and impress you by doing extensive volunteer work with Doctors Without Borders.

"Look, just don't wear heels, ok? We're not actually invited to this party so 20 of us are going to jump the back fence."

She left my cheeseboard selection from my fridge in various places around my apartment. And then denied doing so.

#THE UNHINGED DRUNKARD

I went on a date and forgot what the person looked like when I went to the toilet.

Dates can be stressful, and alcohol is a legal and freely available substance with which you can take the edge off the anxiety. But beyond the point where you shrug off your hang-ups and inhibitions lies a more dangerous stage, where you lose your bearings, your house keys, and your dignity. Your emotions combine to form an unusual and deeply volatile cocktail: misery, aggression, amorousness. Yes, it's true that many relationships begin with excessive drinking, but booze doesn't make anyone more attractive: it just lowers everyone's standards for a period of six hours. And increases everyone's chances of waking up next to someone with whom they share a fondness for shots of flaming sambuca, but precious little else.

He didn't buy me a drink, and spent the whole date talking about himself. He texted me on way home to tell me the radio was playing "our song."

She arrived, saying "I've been in the pub since three." On the word three she fell down the stairs and broke both her stiletto heels.

He disappeared for half an hour to "talk to a guy." When he came back he was surprised to run into me and offered to buy me a drink.

He arrived at my parents' house wearing eyeliner and riding a stolen bicycle, chased by a gang of youths who wanted the bike back.

I went on a date with a Peruvian guy who said to me during our tapas: "You eat like windmill."

One of my dates suggested I guess the length of his penis about, oh, half an hour in. When I demurred he got all "Guess! Just guess!"

A date once took me to a store in Reading where, unbeknownst to me, he shoplifted "Oh Carolina" by Shaggy and then gave it to me as a gift.

I was treated to a 25-minute story about the ins and outs of the baggage handling crisis at Heathrow's Terminal 5.

Arranged a second date with a divorced policeman, who later texted me saying he's not divorced but "wouldn't mind sex" if I was OK with that.

#THE DISGRUNTLED DUMPEE

He had photos of his ex all over his flat, and on our first night he made me watch Dune because she had a bit part in it.

There are various algebraic formulae that people use to estimate how long it should take someone to get over their last relationship. These tend to be slightly optimistic, because no one wants to hear the brutal truth (e.g., eighteen months of gin and tears) when they're feeling that low. But while these formulae never spit out a value of "three weeks," that's how long it takes some types of broken-hearted singletons to decide that they're ready to start dating again. You can spot them during a date by their tendency to start crying while muttering "bitch" or "bastard," as they start using the evening as a comparatively inexpensive form of cognitive behavioral therapy. Also look out for the phrases "But I'm over it now" and "No I'm fine, really," which they're not.

Her first words: "Sorry I'm late. One of the kids at school flooded the toilets and did a big shit in the middle of it."

He claimed he was psychic, knew all the "hidden messages" in Michael Jackson songs and that he had once killed a bison.

His crappy car stalled. I push-started it. He drove off and left me standing in the road. In the rain.

@anonymous

He turned up with one of his "wife's friends."

@redcath

He called 10 minutes before the date to ask if I was running late. He picked a fight with a stranger for looking at him and said aliens are in the Bible.

She thought it would be funny to throw a drink over me as I said I felt a bit hot. It was red wine. I had a white shirt on.

An online date. He arrived, looking nothing like his photos. He was angry with the world. We had an argument about cheese.

She was a conceptual artist who "worked mostly in the medium of knives." Hundreds of sharp, shiny ones in her room.

After the prom, at about 2 am, it was cold and raining. My date refused to give me his jacket because "then I'll be cold."

My date suggested we both bring friends. Within minutes, his friend offered my friend drugs and got angry when she declined.

Third date, he takes me back to his—or rather his dad's place. Which was sheltered housing for the elderly and we had to sneak in.

#THE MACHO POSTURER

He told me he liked to show dogs that he's alpha-male by grabbing their muzzle and staring in their eyes. "It's just how I roll." Not with me it's not.

Assessing exactly how masculine a woman expects a man to be is something that's difficult to calculate—and easy to get wrong, mid-date, as you hoist her over your shoulder in a spirited attempt at a fireman's lift. Some women might prefer their date to look like that poster of a young bodybuilder gently cuddling a baby, with all those caring, nurturing instincts intact, while others might well prefer a close approximation of Mad Max. But making brave stabs in the dark by describing yourself as a bare-knuckle prizefighter when you're actually a tax accountant won't work (see "The Blatant Liar"). Bragging about feats of strength, demonstrating your bench press technique using a golf umbrella, or wrestling a sommelier to the floor are also inadvisable.

@breekom

He said that he'd given up coffee, food and booze, and spent the evening licking sugar from little packets.

@cardio_matters

He corrected my grammar. Repeatedly. When I told him my office is on the Strand, he said "You mean STRAND. No 'The.'"

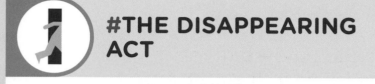

#THE DISAPPEARING ACT

She excused herself after half an hour to go home and check that her cat hadn't set fire to itself on her candles.

Dates can go very wrong very quickly, and it's important to have a getaway plan. The recognized method is to pre-arrange a 9 P.M. text message from a friend summoning you to help them get to hospital after a grisly kitchen accident—but this is so widely used that you may as well say to your date, "I'm sorry, this isn't working." In an ideal world, we'd be honest and open enough to do just that. But instead we invent implausible excuses involving food that we suspect might be going bad in our fridge: trying to be kind, but actually being vaguely insulting. The other approach is to say you're going to the toilet, start walking, and just keep going.

Her opening gambit was that she constantly lied. "Do you want a drink?" I asked. "Yes," she replied. I was confused.

I'm in the back of a cab set for home. He pats the cab firmly and says to the driver: "Drive safely, you have a very precious cargo."

She sprayed Pino Silvestre aftershave on me, linked arms wedding style to drink, and introduced me as her husband.

Her, 30 minutes into our date: "Hope you don't mind, I've brought some friends along." Seven of them, scattered around bar. Bought them drinks.

Once at a concert I met a girl. We went outside. She was cold. I gave her my jacket. She stole my money.

I took him home. During sex, he shouted "I HAVE A WIFE AND CHILD!" It was a bit awkward.

I was once scolded, in all seriousness, and forced to eat ALL my vegetables on a first date.

#THE PARTY ORGANIZER

My date brought a date on the date.

There are occasions when an evening billed as a date turns out to be some kind of social gathering. This could be due to your date being emotionally illiterate, sexually adventurous, or simply preferring to spend time with their friends. But when this scenario transpires around you, even more questions pose themselves. What if I fancy the friend more than my date, and why haven't they considered this? Am I expected to buy a round of drinks? How awkward will this become at the end of the night? But worse than the person who brings a wingman, wingmen, or wingwomen on their date are those who decide to hold some kind of romantic audition to get two, three, or more people ticked off their list. If you find yourself on the dating *X Factor*, quit immediately.

He turned up late, on the phone to a friend. He said to the friend: "I'll call you back in ..." (looked me up and down) "... about 45 minutes."

After one drink she said: "How serious are you?" I stared at her, blankly. She described herself as "80% serious."

She told me how she only dates guys less intelligent than her. In her follow-up text she misspelled "fantastic."

He wanted to "wash up" so removed his shirt. Then said something "bit him" and removed his pants. His friends had told him that women love that.

He asked me to sleep with his best friend, and gave me a Fleetwood Mac CD as a gift so I could learn about "unconventional relationships."

He pretended he was a widower who had lost his wife to cancer. When I became suspicious he said: "She's not dead, exactly."

I thought it was a job interview. He thought it was a date. We both left disappointed.

We went to his family barbecue on a date. His big dog immediately sniffed my crotch, and his dad said "Just like my son, hey boy?"

After one awful date, he went to my workplace, pretended to be a relative to get my address, then turned up at my house.

He asked me: "Will you be my little spoon?" I said no. His follow up: "My big spoon?"

#THE SINSTER CREEP

He spent the evening telling me the best ways to murder people and get away with it.

Ninety-nine percent of bad dates are characterized by mild discomfort, but the remaining one percent can give you a sneaking feeling you might be in mortal danger. Pre-date alarms should sound if it's suggested that you meet in the woods at dusk, or at an industrial park on a Sunday. Stay alert to unusual lines of questioning, such as "Does anyone know where you are right now?" and "How quickly do you think your body might decay?" Also check your escape routes if you hear any stories that end with "…but there was insufficient evidence to link me to that particular crime." Similarly, avoid relentless perspirerers, mouth-breathers, police-lineup resemblers, and dates who stare at parts of your body as if they'd like to put them in freezer bags.

The date ended with him running to a bus stop shouting "I have to go to my friend's cat in Tottenham." We were outside his flat.

I was 18. He took me on a burglary. I stayed in the car, not having a clue what he was doing in that house.

His initials were KJ, and he insisted I call him Cagey. He then warned me that his ex would put a Wiccan curse on us.

He wore bicycle clips throughout and made a scene with the restaurant staff about the size of portions for the price.

He tried to storm out of my apartment when I said I wasn't interested. Then had to come back for me to unlock the door.

He told me he was 30, but was actually 37. He didn't want to attract a woman "over 29 and therefore on the shelf."

He asked if I was OK with him turning up when he wanted, but not contacting me between visits. He also insisted I learn piano.

#THE SEXUAL DEVIANT

> *He showed up at the restaurant with crutches for me to hop around on later on, as it turned him on. I faked a migraine and left.*

In the context of a long-term relationship, it's surprising how many mild perversions can be politely accommodated. So I've heard. But to confess them as an opening gambit suggests that their compulsion to, say, fondle furniture, or auto-asphyxiate with tropical fruit, is more important to them than getting along with someone on a more fundamental level. And maybe that's true. But they can't be surprised if people react badly— particularly if it's mentioned in a matter-of-fact way that suggests everyone is doing it, and we're the prudes for not wanting to introduce tortoises into love-play, or whatever. Then again, dating is a percentage game. It's possible that this strategy works once in every two hundred attempts. And that would end up being one hell of a night.

I went on a date with a woman who had pre-arranged for two other men to meet her at the same time and location.

He actually said: "But enough about me, let's talk about you." Without a hint of irony.

He spent the whole date mocking teaching (I teach) then said the date hadn't been worth the price of his train ticket.

He kept making gun signs at me, shouting "Who's your daddy?"

She stubbed a cigarette out on the back of my hand. After asking to. And me saying no.

Went on a date, no chemistry, didn't call her. Years later I saw her on a TV makeover show, saying that she'd only been on one date in her whole life.

@sitemanagergal

30 minutes into a first date his mobile rings. He answered. "Hi Mom! Yeah, I'm with her now. It's great. Put Dad on, I'll tell him."

He showed up to meet me in a bar in full fencing garb, carrying his wallet in his face protector thing.

He lived at home. I had to sneak past his mom, who was my favorite teacher when I was 10, and I found a large knife under his bed.

The date went well until he mentioned his name is not really Steven, nor was he 27, nor single.

#THE TACTLESS IDIOT

He said: "This lunch could only be improved if I was eating it with a beautiful woman."

When we're nervous, we say stupid things. We blurt out idle thoughts that social convention and common sense would normally force us to suppress—for instance, expressing disappointment at the size of your date's breasts, or the severity of their receding hairline. Dates should be sprinkled with light pleasantries as you pay compliments and show general interest, even if it requires you to dredge up superhuman levels of effort and ingenuity. Yes, it may feel like hard work, but it's better than being brutally honest and digging yourself into a pit of embarrassment as a result. Of course, if you've decided that a) you want to make a sharp exit and b) the best way of doing so is to make your date hate you, then yes, tactless idiocy is one way to go. But it won't enhance your reputation.

I invited the guy over for dinner, he asked if he could take a shower, then told me he'd wanked in it.

Fifteen minutes into the date, he said "If I was my friend Michael I'd do this—" and promptly grabbed my tits.

He asked me if I wanted to go back to his place to look at his plants. We did. He had a house full of plants. Then I left.

He insisted I pay for dinner as I made more money than him. He then said: "You may make more money, but I'm better looking."

I am living proof that the line "I can't see you anymore, I'm becoming a priest" is still in modern use. After one date.

He took a phone call and said "about seven?" He then pretended that "seven" was the number of people he'd interviewed that day.

A guy I used to work with asked me out. He seemed really nice whilst in the office but on the first date he kicked a pigeon.

@RX2904

She insisted on me going to Tibet with her to save the monks. When I said I don't want to, she said "Yes, you do."

@sarah_j_bond

I spent an evening taking a hat round to collect money whilst he breakdanced (badly) until we had enough money for a drink and a KFC.

He kept an overly large coat on throughout. The reason became clear when he stole my handbag while I was in the toilet.

We chatted for months at work. We finally went for lunch on Xmas Eve. Holding hands, she told me that she was spending Xmas with her husband.

#THE DELUDED OPTIMIST

Lunch date with a fellow mall employee. He says, "You know that outfit you wore the other day? I prefer that. Keep it in mind."

For these people, a first date is not an exploratory venture, but an indication of firm commitment for an extended period of weeks, months, or even years. Presenting the relationship as a fait accompli, they combat their colossal insecurity by making hopeful, positive statements like "Well, I think this is going well, don't you?" before you've even sat down. This is probably the polar opposite of "playing it cool"; the delicate dance of courtship is ruined as they effectively push a document across the table toward you for a countersignature. "Your place or mine" is the mildest manifestation of deluded optimism; "I'll grab a few things and then move the rest of my belongings in a bit later in the week" is among the most extreme.

@scarletwestend

His first question: "Would you rather burn to death, drown, or be buried alive?"

@ninbats

He told me that when he showered he often fantasized that it was a golden shower, and once considered telling his grandmother.

@djcollyer

While waiting for my date I met a different girl at the bar. I bought her a drink. My date arrived. I tried to pretend I wasn't me.

@BettyKitten

In a crowded pub he loudly exclaimed that he was very good at cunnilingus, then showed me topless phone snaps of his sister.

"Lovely evening," I said, "but I'm not interested." He grabbed me, stuck his tongue down my throat, and stood back saying "AND NOW?"

We discovered we had a mutual acquaintance. I said, "He's a great guy." She said "He stabbed my brother."

He told me how he once did a giant poo over a fence next to the freeway. "No kidding, it was the size of a wine bottle."

He professed a love of James Bond, and suggested a reconstruction of the white bikini scene. While demonstrating his JB "sexy face."

After rebuffing his advances, he said: "I would say 'Get home safe,' but frankly I don't give a fuck."

#THE TIMID CREATURE

I went to install a modem for a woman I met. Wasn't sure if it was a date or technical support. Got a check, chatted awkwardly on her bed, left.

The most astonishing thing about these fragile waifs is how they ever mustered up the courage to venture out on a date in the first place. So unsure of themselves that they have trouble uttering their own name, they frequently sit in panic-stricken silence, speaking only to confirm that yes, they are enjoying themselves really. Trembling, sweating, shaking, stuttering, and unexpectedly urinating are classic behaviors, as is an inability to hold your gaze for more than a fraction of a second. Holding hands would cause them to pass out; sexual contact would threaten the operation of their entire central nervous system. They may inspire sympathy, but a relationship built upon sympathy is doomed. It's not an exam, after all. It's just a date.

He came to get me in his new Porsche. Before I got in he put a towel on my seat because "girls can sometimes be sweaty down there."

@acraigfots

She opened with "my boyfriend isn't happy about this." Then he called her. Twice. Then he turned up and they had a massive fight.

During light conversation prior to dinner my date mentions casually that she likes to "fuck" in a Nazi uniform she made.

He gave me $20 bills to get myself something from every shop. He kept the change. Turned out the bills were fake.

I once phoned a date to ask why he was late, or if he needed directions. He said he was busy doing "hundreds of pushups."

He spent 20 minutes explaining how to get on and off a ski lift with a snowboard. I hadn't actually asked.

She said "I really hoped you'd be someone else" and left.

On my last date the guy had a pet wooden giraffe that had its own Facebook page. His name was Sebastian. (The giraffe.)

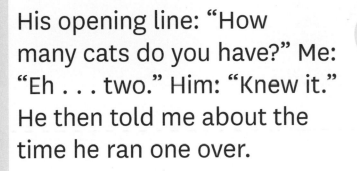

His opening line: "How many cats do you have?" Me: "Eh . . . two." Him: "Knew it." He then told me about the time he ran one over.

Dull evening, no chemistry. Walking to the subway, he announces: "I'm finding it so hard to walk with this erection."

#THE CHARMLESS CHEAPSKATE

Me: "Let's split the bill."
Him: "I should think so too;
my mom didn't burn her bra
so women like you could get
a free meal."

Paying for the cost of a night out should be simple. You either go halves, or one of you displays a bit of unexpected generosity and offers to pay for the lot. And you then have the back-and-forth "No, you mustn't" / "Yes, I insist" argument. Disagreement over excessive generosity is perfectly permissible in the book of modern social etiquette, but arguments over lack of it are, by contrast, excruciating. "No, you had the steak and that cost more than my fish" is a gigantic signpost informing you that a relationship with this person would mean joyless belt-tightening and an incessant counting of loose change. Everyone has a budget, of course—the problem occurs when you produce the budget from your pocket and start waving it about, complaining loudly.

My date kept talking about his love of Woody Woodpecker cartoons, describing several episodes in excruciating detail.

I refused a kiss goodnight so he asked if he could see my ass instead. I said no thanks.

Him: "I like filtering people on dating websites. I would never date an Indian girl, for example."
Me: "I'm half-Indian."

Halfway through the date he paused and said "I'm sorry, I have absolutely no idea what your name is." Sigh.

@NicholasPassant

Took a date to bed, where she denied the Holocaust.

@MissHEB

My friend invited her date over for a cup of tea. When she brought in tea and biscuits he had his penis in his hand. He said: "Don't you like it?"

I'm 4'11". Went on date with a 6'4" guy. He said he felt like he was with his daughter. Then I spilt pasta sauce down my top.

As the appetizers arrived in an Indian restaurant, she said "I'm going to leave, you're drawing too much attention by being fat."

He asked me at dinner if my breasts were real. He said he would only date me if they were implants. Told him he would never know.

The guy had a remote vibrator with him and suggested I go to the bathroom and put it on so that he could control it remotely.

@algae

Detour via the prison before dinner. To bail out his brother. Who'd stabbed his girlfriend.

He wouldn't let me get out of the car until I finished listening to a Simply Red song. He reached across and held the door shut.

I escaped from a morning-after situation by joining an animal rights march, shouting "This is important to me."

I once agreed to have dinner with my boss, where he addressed me as "my little mouse." "Would my little mouse like a glass of wine?"

He was an exchange student. He took 25 minutes and a Spanish-English dictionary to ask if he could take a "sensual picturegraph" of me. I declined.

Me: "So, what do you like to do?" Him: "I actually have quite a significant porn collection."

He turned up with two shopping bags stuffed full of toilet rolls. He told me he'd nicked them from his work.

@l_a_coaster

He insisted I feed him at lunch and at the movies by smacking his lips together and leaning toward me.

@Katie_Reynolds

Realizing he wasn't going to get laid, he chatted up a random girl on a pedestrian crossing, ditched me, and went off with her.

@BruceRenny

There was the woman into whose handbag I accidentally tipped a pint of steaming hot onion gravy.

@JessicaRoseJRv

One boy texted me the complete lyrics to "Hit Me Baby One More Time," replacing the word "hit" with "text." I did not respond.

@ChristineCarr

On date two, he told me EXACTLY the same stories as on date one. Like following a script. I began chipping in, and he said we were "so in tune."

I said "So, how big is America then?" to an American.

@CaraWilsonEssex

He didn't speak nor make eye contact. When he did finally speak his words were "I could be watching football."

Went out with a guy who sent me a scanner pic of his penis the next day, squashed against the glass, with his number written on it.

He admitted he had been in prison, unraveled his socks to reveal drugs, then asked if I wanted a loan. I was 18.

He thought it would be fun to sneak up behind me and give me a fright when we met. I thought he was a bag-snatcher and punched him.

He wouldn't take his hat off as he'd just had a hair transplant.

He told me that if I wanted to ask a question I had to say "Please, Sir." He then ordered a peach schnapps & lemon.

He couldn't remember or pronounce my name, so he asked if I would mind if he just called me Amy instead.

He said women should cook. I said what if I work longer hours and come home late? He said "I'd wait."

He took me to Taco Bell and showed me his tattoos of Sonic the Hedgehog and the state of Ohio.

My date introduced me to her boyfriend, then apologized because she didn't think he'd be there.

He took me to dinner. No chemistry & little conversation. He kept saying "Bet you can't wait for this to be over, can you?"

Acknowledgments

Many thanks to Jenny McIvor, Tim Bates, Rory Scarfe, Julian Flanders, Craig Stevens, Steve Mockus, Walter C. Baumann, Courtney Drew, Emily Dubin, Becca Boe, and everyone who shared their traumatic dating stories. If you'd like to share your own, please do! Either visit www.crapdates.co.uk or tweet your story to @FirstDateHell.

About the Author

Rhodri Marsden writes for the *Independent* newspaper, plays in far too many bands, and is a connoisseur of crap dates. He lives in London.